D0821484

OUTDOOR SPORTS SKILLS

HOW TO CAMP LIKE A PRO

JEFF BURLINGAME

Library of Congress Cataloging-in-Publication Data

Burlingame, Jeff.
How to camp like a pro / Jeff Burlingame.
pages cm. — (Outdoor sports skills)
Includes bibliographical references and index.
Summary: "In this 'How-to' guide, learn the basic skills and necessities of camping including how to set up camp, what supplies to bring, and how to have safe and fun adventures"—Provided by publisher.
ISBN 978-1-62285-239-0
1. Camping—Handbooks, manuals, etc.—Juvenile literature. I. Title.
GV191.7.B87 2015
796.54—dc23
2014001215

Future editions:
Paperback ISBN: 978-1-62285-240-6
EPUB ISBN: 978-1-62285-241-3
Single-User PDF ISBN: 978-1-62285-242-0
Multi-User PDF ISBN: 978-1-62285-243-7

Printed in the United States of America
052014 Lake Book Manufacturing, Inc., Melrose Park, IL
10 9 8 7 6 5 4 3 2 1

To Our Readers: We have done our best to make sure all Internet addresses in this book were active and appropriate when we went to press. However, the author and the publisher have no control over and assume no liability for the material available on those Internet sites or on other Web sites they may link to. Any comments or suggestions can be sent by e-mail to comments@speedingstar.com or to the address below:

Speeding Star
Box 398, 40 Industrial Road
Berkeley Heights, NJ 07922
USA
www.speedingstar.com

Enslow Publishers, Inc., is committed to printing our books on recycled paper. The paper in every book contains 10% to 30% post-consumer waste (PCW). The cover board on the outside of each book contains 100% PCW. Our goal is to do our part to help young people and the environment too!

Illustration Credits: Library of Congress: p. 13; ©Thinkstock: (JupiterimagesCollection/Stockbyte, p. 7; Brett HillyardCollection/iStock, p. 8; Thinkstock ImagesCollection:Stockbyte, p. 23; Design Pics, 41); Shutterstock: (©Kondrachov Vladimir, p.4; ©maga, pp.5, 14; ©Nigel Paul Monckton, p. 6; ©oliveromg, pp. 11, 25; ©Matt Ragen, p. 12; ©Mark Herreid, p. 17; ©Dan Kosmayer, p. 19: ©Photoseeker, p. 20; ©kabby, p.21; ©jdwfoto, p. 27; ©Lisa F. Young, p. 28; ©Africa Studio, p. 30; ©Friday Ivo, p. 31; ©Elena Rostunova, p. 32; ©PlusONE, p. 33; ©Blend Images, p. 35; ©Harvepino, p. 36; ©HABRDA, p. 37; ©Dave Allen Photography, p. 39; ©auremar, p. 42; ©Anja Peternelj, p. 45).

Cover Illustration: ©Thinkstock: JupiterimagesCollection/Stockbyte

CONTENTS

FUNDAMENTALS

The stars are shining overhead. Boisterous crickets are chirping in the nearby grass. Your clock says it is way before your normal summer-break bedtime, yet the near-black sky and your tired body say differently. Tomorrow comes early when you're sleeping outdoors, especially when you know that tomorrow will be full of amazing adventures. Should you take a sight-seeing trip to the beach? How about a mind-clearing hike through the mountains? And no matter what, there will be an end-of-the-warm-day dip in the glacier-fed lake. So many possibilities.

So you stow away the graham crackers and marshmallows, gather a bucket of water to help your parents douse the campfire, and shovel dirt on top of the steaming coals to make sure there's no chance of the flames reigniting overnight. Then you enter your tent or camper, snuggle into your

On a clear night, the stars in the sky become the center of attention.

One of the most enjoyable experiences of camping is being able to cook meals over an open flame.

sleeping bag, and—quickly—you are safe, sound, and snoring.

Each year, more than 43 million Americans do what you are doing. For many of those people, vacationing in the great outdoors has been a family tradition for decades. For others, it may be the first time they have traded in their ovens for the open flames of the peaceful, primitive activity called camping.

WHAT IS CAMPING?

Choosing to leave one's house to recreate and sleep outdoors is the essence of camping. Exactly where you choose to camp or what you sleep in when you are doing so can vary greatly. Most American campers participate in what is called car camping. It is an activity that is exactly what it sounds like. Car campers typically fill their vehicles with supplies—including tents and sleeping bags to sleep in, clothes, and food to eat and a means of cooking it—and drive to a location of their choice. Once they get there, they set up camp close to their cars. The cars become sort of

Some campers set up camp close to their car, so the car can act as a home base.

These campers are enjoying their campsite .

a home base, and are available for travel to and from whatever destination you and your fellow campers choose to visit.

The process of setting up camp commonly includes unpacking and erecting a tent, unpacking food, clothes, and bedding from the car, and cleaning and preparing an eating area.

Some people drive for several hours or even days to get to their camping locations. Others who are fortunate enough to live in or nearby areas fit for exploration prefer to stay closer to home. Regardless of how far they travel, most campers have one thing in common: they choose to stay in public campgrounds. Public campgrounds can be found all around the United States. Many are located in local, state, or national

A camper eats dinner at a primitve campsite in Yosemite National Park, California.

parks. Others, such as the popular Kampgrounds of America [KOA] chain, are privately owned. This means they are not funded by the government.

Both public and private campgrounds typically charge campers a small daily fee to camp at their locations. In exchange for the payment, campers receive use of a certain section of land for their campsite, as well as access to other amenities such as community rest rooms, running water, showers, picnic tables, and more.

In addition to car camping, there are several other ways to camp. Some people prefer to sleep in cabins rather than tents. Cabins are more expensive than tent sites, but they provide ready-made shelter and thus are less work. Many public and private campgrounds offer cabins for rent. Recreational vehicles [RVs] are another popular camping option, and permanent tent-like structures called yurts also can be found at many locations.

A more advanced form of camping is called primitive camping. Primitive campers typically carry their supplies in large backpacks and hike for short or long distances on backcountry trails where motorized vehicles are not allowed. Primitive campsites offer fewer amenities than do car campsites. Some primitive campsites offer no amenities at all, not even water or rest room facilities. Primitive camping takes more advanced planning than car camping, and some knowledge of wilderness survival skills also is necessary. First-time primitive campers should always travel with at least one experienced partner.

LOCATION IS EVERYTHING

Regardless of the type of campsite you choose to stay at, one thing is just about certain: Your campsite will be located at or near an area where outdoor activities are common. It may be located on a warm lake or a quick-moving river. It may be next to an ocean or in the foothills of a snow-capped mountain, or nearby a popular national park. It may even have a swimming pool and a small grocery store.

Unless, of course, you are among the many young campers who decide to stay at home—literally. Each year, thousands of children drag their tents just outside their own back doors to camp in the backyard. Doing so is a great way to practice camping skills with the safety and supervision of mom and dad just a short walk away.

HISTORY OF CAMPING

People have been using tents as a means of shelter for thousands of years. But it was not until the late 19th century that it became popular to do so recreationally. A British tailor by the name of Thomas Hiram Holding often has been given credit for making that so. Holding spent many years traveling throughout England, Scotland, Ireland, The United States, and elsewhere. His first camping experience came was when he was nine years old, when he and three hundred other people camped along the Mississippi River.

Holding often traveled with little more than a canoe and a pack full of supplies. Those supplies included a small tent, which he would erect each evening using

DID YOU KNOW?

In America, camping is the most popular vacationing activity done outdoors.

Camping locally is a good test to measure if you can handle roughing it in the wilderness.

rope and a couple of well-placed poles. In 1908, Holding published *The Camper's Handbook*. The book was full of stories and tips he had collected during his years of camping. Many of the camping tips in Holding's book still are good ones today.

The Boy Scouts of America have their own campgrounds where they provide nothing more than the basic essentials.

PRO TIPS AND TRICKS

When not using a flashlight, put the batteries in backward so that it cannot be turned on accidentally. Not having a flashlight could turn into a really big problem if the campfire goes out or if you need to walk to the bathroom at night!

Camping is a part of Girl Scout tradition. Here a Girl Scout cooks over an open fire about 1920.

By the time *The Camper's Handbook* was published, several campsites already had sprung up across the United States. Many groups—such as the Young Men's Christian Association [YMCA], Young Women's Christian Association [YWCA], Boy Scouts and Girl Scouts—began using camping as a teaching tool and a way for their members to gather and have fun. As those youths grew to have families of their own, they took their children camping, too.

Camping's popularity continued to grow over the years, and more and more campsites were created to meet the growing demand. Today, tens of millions of Americans go camping every year. The reasons they choose to do so are as varied as the campers themselves.

PRO TIPS AND TRICKS

Hiking can cause blisters on the bottoms of the feet. To help prevent this from happening, take a bar of soap and rub it along the inside your socks, mainly on the toes and the heel.

Instead of TVs and cell phones, campers watch a crackling fire and gaze at the stars in the night sky. Many find out that the sights of nature are even more exciting.

WHY GO CAMPING?

In *The Camper's Handbook*, author Thomas Holding spent an entire page listing the reasons he believed people loved to camp:

- "It keeps old men young."
- "It affords rest of mind."
- "It gives young people experience that they would not [otherwise] have."
- "It is an educational force, which would take a chapter to describe."

Most of the reasons Holding listed more than one-hundred years ago still are reasons people enjoy camping today. Camping allows people to experience nature without the hustle and bustle of everyday life. It allows them to spend quality time with friends and family, away from the television, and other forms of technology. Camping affords the opportunity to visit new places and appreciate the many wonders nature has to offer.

The relatively low cost is another reason people choose to camp. Camping is the perfect choice for many budget-conscious travelers. The cost of one night's stay in a hotel can be greater than the cost of several nights at a campground. And many campgrounds allow pets, too. It is difficult to find hotels that allow pets, but when you choose to go camping, even Fido and Fifi can come along and enjoy in the fun. Camping is an adventure the whole family can participate in.

SUPPLIES

Preparing to camp—especially for the first time—does take some planning. Even the most experienced campers occasionally forget to pack an item or two. If those items happen to be important ones such as sleeping bags or tents, even the most otherwise-perfect camping trip can turn into a headache. Especially if you are camping far away from shops and stores. But there is one way to make sure you don't forget a single item. It is called a camping checklist and it is easy to prepare.

MAKING A CHECKLIST, CHECKING IT TWICE

Exactly what your checklist will contain depends on what type of camping you will be doing. Those who are sleeping in semi-furnished cabins with electricity, for example, will need different supplies than those who are sleeping in tents in the middle of a sprawling national park. But regardless of your destination, there are some important items most everyone can agree upon that need to be brought in order to make the most of your camping adventure. These items include:

- ***A tent***. Tents come in many sizes and styles. Your parents can help determine which one is right for your family. Most tents come stored in a bag that contains everything you need to set the tent up in most conditions. However, a hammer can

Besides a tent, a sleeping bag is the most important supply to bring on a camping trip.

be helpful to pound tent stakes into the ground, and a tarp or thick cloth will help keep the bottom of your tent (and possibly your bedding!) from becoming moist from the ground. Tents with porches or awnings do the best job of keeping the dirt out.

- ***Bedding***. Those camping in areas where it tends to get chilly at night need more bedding than those who are sleeping in areas where the temperature remains moderate. But for tent camping, a basic

DID YOU KNOW?

Matches can be made waterproof by dipping them in nail polish or paraffin wax.

sleeping bag is a necessity. A pillow, just as it is at home, is another must-have. Air mattresses, sleeping pads, or extra blankets can help soften your sleeping surface if you place them under your sleeping bag.

- ***Clothes.*** This may seem obvious, but the clothes you need for camping may not be the same ones you would need at home on a daily basis. A hat to protect the head from the sun (or the rain—but hopefully not!) is one important item many campers forget to bring. Rain gear can be similarly vital if there's a chance of precipitation, and hiking boots are necessary if you plan to take part in that fun activity. Other clothing items that should be considered for a camping checklist include pants, belts, T-shirts, socks, underwear, pajamas, swim suits, towels, shorts, and more. A laundry bag to store dirty clothes also will come in handy, and is another item many campers forget.
- ***Kitchen supplies and food.*** Because your parents likely will be doing the cooking, it is best to have them prepare or at least oversee this portion of your

PRO TIPS AND TRICKS

A slight breeze is all it takes for a tent to get destroyed. Make sure the tent is staked down to the ground to help prevent problems from occurring. To add further support, put heavy rocks on the inside corners of the tent to hold it down.

When it comes to camping, some feel the most important foods to bring are graham crackers, marshmallows, and chocolate.

checklist. Common kitchen supplies include cups, plates, bowls, utensils, pans, an ice cooler, a charcoal or propane grill, dish soap, paper towels, trash bags, plastic bags, and a can opener. Food choices vary, depending on taste. In general, easy-to-prepare items—such as hot dogs, hamburgers, salads, and sandwiches—are the best options. Just don't forget the marshmallows.

- ***First-aid kit***. Unfortunately, injuries sometimes occur in nature. Thus, packing a standard first-aid kit to treat such things as bug bites and stings, minor cuts and scrapes, burns, and sprains is crucial.

It is important to have an alternate light source, such as a battery-powered lantern.

- ***Personal items.*** The needs of each individual camper vary. Soap, shampoo, deodorant, toilet paper, toothpaste and toothbrush, and hairbrushes are some common items that should be included on this portion of the checklist. Personal medications are perhaps the most important item that should be listed here.
- ***Miscellaneous.*** This part of the checklist is also known as the "Do you really need to bring that?" section. Sometimes, the answer will be "yes." Some of those "yes" items on camping trips might include a camera, batteries, an alarm clock, a flashlight, a pocketknife, sunscreen, books and magazines, and fishing gear. Which items are a "yes" and which ones are a "no" depends on the person—and oftentimes how much room you have in your pack. Everyone's miscellaneous list is different.

There are several spots online where you can find camping checklists that can be printed out and customized to meet your specific needs. The most important part of a checklist is to make sure you have one. You should fill it out several days prior to your trip. Hang it on the refrigerator, and check off each item as you pack it. There is nothing worse than arriving at a far-off place and realizing you forgot an essential item, such as a pan to cook with, for example. With a little checklist-preparation time, you won't forget anything, and your camping adventure will be a much better one.

It is always better to over pack than it is to under pack.

SETTING UP CAMP

If camping seems like a lot of work, that is because it can be. Especially the first couple times you do it. Thankfully, one of camping's busiest times is over with shortly after you arrive at your destination. That busy time is setting up your camp.

When you first arrive at your campground, you will need to check in with the campground's host. In state and national parks, that host is often a park ranger. At private campgrounds such as KOAs, the host will be the campground owners, or someone who works for them. Whoever the host is, he or she will give you basic information about your location. They will tell you where your campsite is, how to get there, the rules of the campground, and answer any other questions you may have.

Some campgrounds are first-come, first-serve. At those places, all campsites are available to everyone

PRO TIPS AND TRICKS

Being able to start a fire can be tough to do, especially if it is wet or windy outside. Put petroleum jelly on cotton balls to use as a fire starter. Another good trick is to take a toilet paper roll and stuff it with dryer lint. Both tricks will help get a fire going in no time!

After the tent is pitched, finish unpacking and get situated.

until they are filled. Other campgrounds work on a reservation system, where campers book their campsites days, weeks, or months in advance either online, in person, or over the telephone. Reserving in advance allows campers the ability to guarantee that the site they want is available to them when they arrive. Some campers may prefer to be near the bathroom, while others may prefer to be off in a secluded area so they can get away from it all.

The size and features of campsites vary from location to location. Most campsites are relatively small, especially compared to the size of the average person's house. So it is important to be as efficient and tidy as possible when organizing a campsite.

TENT TIME

Once you've arrived at your campsite, it's time to unpack. Tents should be the first thing you set up, because they are most likely where everything else in your car will eventually be stored. Find a flat spot of ground—and preferably also a dry and soft one. If you are camping somewhere warm, try to find a shady spot for your tent. Then, lay your tarp or cloth down, and erect your tent over top of it.

Setting up a tent is fairly easy, though it can be somewhat confusing the first couple times you try it. Reading the instructions prior to the trip and setting up the tent a couple of times in your backyard will help speed things up when it comes time for your camping adventure.

These young women have successfully set up camp. Their tents are on a flat spot of ground.

After the tent is set up, it is time to set up your sleeping arrangements. After all, comfortable sleeping is the main purpose for having a tent! Otherwise, you could just sleep on the ground. Inflate your air mattress or roll out your padding into the bottom of the tent, then position your and your tentmate(s) sleeping bags and pillows inside. Now is a good time to bring other items into your tent, as well, such as clothing, alarm clocks, and flashlights for those unavoidable nighttime trips to the rest room.

Following, and making sure others follow, two important tent rules will make your experience more enjoyable. First, always remove your shoes before entering the tent. This will help keep dirt out. Second, always zip your tent when you are done entering and exiting it. This will help keep bugs out. Nothing is worse than a 2:00 A.M. wake-up call from Mister Mosquito, except a first-thing-in-the-morning trip to the first-aid kit to find something to help soothe the itchiness of Mister Mosquito's bite. Keep the tent clean, and you will be less likely to have to worry about such headaches.

COOKING AND EATING AREA

After the tents are done, it is time to focus on the cooking and eating area. Because this area often involves open flames (and smoke), it is important to keep it as far away from your tent and foliage as possible. Most campsites have fire pits and picnic tables that can be used as visual clues as to where your cooking and eating area should be. Some campsites even come with built-in, elevated grills. Most fire pits

Some campgrounds will supply grills at each campsite, but most won't provide charcoal.

also have cooking grates. Whether you cook with one of the supplied means or with your own propane stove or grill is up to you.

Water is the most vital component of any campsite. In the cooking and eating area, it will be used for drinking, food preparation, dish washing, cleaning, and more. Campgrounds often have numerous faucets where campers can obtain quality drinking water.

Campers choosing more primitive sites that do not have water must either bring their own or find a natural water source from which to get it. Water from those natural sources—such as lakes or streams—must be purified in some way before it is consumed.

The first step is to clean and sanitize the cooking and eating area. If it is the picnic table you chose to dine on, use a plastic tablecloth to cover it. If the campers before you were clean, there shouldn't be much cleaning to do. But be sure to clean anyway.

Always clean up immediately following a meal. Nothing will lure insects and other animals such as birds, raccoons, squirrels, and even bears out of hiding quicker than unattended food. Wrap all food and place it back in its appropriate storage container when you are done with it. Wash dishes immediately, either using a designated dish-washing area or in a large bowl filled with hot soapy water. Obtain the hot water by boiling it in a pan over the fire or on a stove. Do not dump the dirty dishwater on vegetation.

Pick up and dispose of all garbage when you are done eating and cleaning. It is important to remember

Campers who leave food behind can be sure raccoons and other animals will smell it and invade the campsite.

PRO TIPS AND TRICKS

No one is perfect, and at the same time, no one likes to clean more than necessary. To help keep animals away from your campsite, store, cook, and eat all food away from the sleeping area. That way, if a mess is made, at least the animals won't be visting right next to the tent!

you are in staying in the habitat of many animals. You are in their home. Leaving food of any kind out is an open invitation to such animals. Many of those animals, such as coyotes and bears, can be dangerous and you want to keep them as far away from your campsite as possible.

CAMPFIRE PREPARATION

Sitting around the fire—singing songs, roasting marshmallows, and spending time with friends and family—is one of the best parts of camping. But before you can do so, a bit of preparation is necessary. Most importantly, campfires need wood. Some campers choose to bring their own firewood. Those people either buy it in bundles from stores or roadside stands, or haul it from home in a trailer or, if there's room, inside their car or truck. Other campers purchase their wood from the campground. In some locations, it is even OK to forage for wood in the areas around your campsite. Sometimes, previous campers are kind enough to leave their leftover firewood for the next person to use. Once you have obtained your wood, stack it near the spot where you intend to build your fire.

Always make sure you have adult supervision when building a fire. Never use gasoline or other combustible liquids to start a fire, and never leave a fire unattended once you get it going. At the end of the evening, when everyone is heading to bed, use water to make sure every last glowing coal is extinguished.

Some campgrounds do not allow campfires. This is especially true in campgrounds where forest fires are likely. Many campgrounds that do allow campfires limit them to built-in fire rings. If there is any question as to whether a fire is permitted at your site, check with campground officials before starting one.

Most overnight camping trips will not need more than one or two bundles of wood.

DID YOU KNOW?

The closer a campsite is to a body of water, the chances of insects being around gets higher.

To make a campfire as safe as possible, make sure it is built on top of sand and surrounded with rocks.

CAMPGROUND ETIQUETTE

It is extremely important to remember you are not alone at your campground. At some campgrounds, there may be hundreds of others camping at the same time as you. Many campgrounds have rules in place to make sure everyone's stay is as comfortable as possible. Most campgrounds also have quiet hours, times where people are expected to be quiet so others can sleep. Typical quiet hours are 9:00 P.M.–7:00 A.M.

STAY SAFE

The great outdoors offers some unique challenges when it comes to staying safe and healthy. The Centers for Disease Control and Prevention offers several tips designed to protect campers. They include:

- Get vaccinated before you travel.
- Prepare healthy and safe food by making sure it is stored at the proper temperature, prepared on clean surfaces, and cooked thoroughly.
- Protect against carbon monoxide poisoning. The odorless and colorless gas found in gas stoves, lanterns, and other devices can be deadly. Never use such devices inside your tent or in areas without adequate ventilation.

It is always important to watch how loud you get in a campground because neighboring campers may be fairly close by.

Lifejackets are designed to keep things afloat. So anyone participating in a water activity should always wear one as a safety precaution.

- Avoid contact with wild animals.
- Always wear bug repellent.
- Use sunscreen and drink plenty of fluids.
- Wear a life jacket when participating in water activities.

Following these important and simple rules will make you camping trip safer.

ADVENTURE TIME

Preparing for a camping trip and setting up camp is at the same time both a lot of work and a lot of fun. After the prep work is done and the campsite is ready to go, a small percentage of campers choose to spend the rest of their trip enjoying the fruits of that labor. According to The Outdoor Foundation, nearly two out of every ten campers do not participate in any other outdoor activity during their trip. They spend their days relaxing at their campsite, playing card games, reading books, cooking, and conversing.

But for the other 80 percent, or eight out of every ten campers—the vast majority—camping is a considered a "gateway" through which to participate in other types of outdoor fun.

HIKING

In one survey conducted by The Outdoor Foundation, most people said hiking was their favorite activity to do while camping. That is because it is by far the easiest activity to do. Hikes—walking to sightsee and for fun—can be long or short. They can take place in flower-filled parks, through hilly, old-growth forests, or on warm, waterlogged beaches. They can be done over flat or hilly surfaces, in meadows, or along riverbeds. Campers can hike alone or with large groups. Hiking is one of the

DID YOU KNOW?

Tents aren't cheap and they definitely should be taken care of to give them longer use. Set up tents on top of a tarp or another type of ground cover to help prevent moisture inside the tent.

Don't settle for only participating in the relaxation aspect of camping. Pursue other outdoor activities while you are there. Explore!

Some people like to camp in places where they can explore and sightsee.

best ways to experience nature as well as the company of those you are camping with.

Little equipment is needed for short hikes, and just about anyone can do them. More advanced hikers carry large backpacks filled with gear and often travel dozens of miles over several days. But the majority of hikers choose to hike for only hours or minutes. If you're camping in a state or national park, it is a safe bet that there are several groomed hiking trails available near where you are. Most of those trails are well-marked and well-maintained.

At the beginning of each hike—an area called a trailhead—there will be signs that tell how long the trail is, how steep it is, and oftentimes how long it will take you to travel it. Some trails are loops which circle around to end where they began. Others are out-and-back trails, which means you'll be hiking to your destination and back on the exact same path.

It is important to stay on designated trails when hiking to minimize damage to vegetation.

FISHING

Fishing is another favorite activity of campers. Like hiking, there are several different types of fishing. Most of them require a license for people over a certain age,

Depending on how serious of a camper you are, you may go camping with the intention of fishing for dinner.

DID YOU KNOW?

Keep a tin can handy when you go camping. It can be used as a pan to cook on.

and there are other rules and regulations that need to be followed, too. Those rules vary from area to area, so a little research is necessary for those campers who think they might want to fish during their trip.

Once the details are figured out, fishing can provide hours of enjoyment, and—for those who are lucky—some food to cook for dinner. Freshwater fishing is done on lakes and streams. Saltwater fishing is fishing that is done on the ocean. Fishing poles and bait or tackle are generally the only required pieces of equipment necessary to fish. Exactly what type of pole to use varies by area. For the best advice—and the best chance to land a fish—ask a camp ranger or someone familiar with the area what gear they use before you head out.

Many fishermen and fisherwomen do so just for the fun of it, and do not bring the fish home with them. Rather, they practice a technique called catch and release. Catch and release is considered an environmentally friendly way to fish. It involves hooking a fish and then gently releasing it back into the water alive.

PHOTOGRAPHY

Nature photography always has been a popular pastime for many people. The recent rise in popularity of digital cameras and cell phones with cameras has made it even more so. There is no better place to practice the art of photography than on a camping trip, where subjects are all around you. Birds are flying over your head and squirrels are scurrying from your picnic table back to the top of a tree. Your friends are jumping into

PRO TIPS AND TRICKS

In the event it starts raining during your trip, make sure to set up camp on flat ground and away from dry water beds. Being in a possible water path could ruin a trip in a matter of minutes.

Bringing a camera or a cell phone that can take pictures while camping is smart because sometimes nature provides a great photo opportunity. This is Grandfather Mountain in the mountains of North Carolina.

PRO TIPS AND TRICKS

It can get cold sleeping outside, especially after the sun goes down. When setting up camp, position the tent to face where the sun will rise so it can warm you up immediately.

a swimming hole and seedlings are breaking ground amongst blackened tree stumps left over from a decades-old forest fire. Photo opportunities are endless when you're camping. All you have to do is look around.

WATER ACTIVITIES

A majority of American families take their camping trips during the summer, when school is on break and the weather is sunny. In many areas of the country, summer is the only time of the year to—warmly, at least—have fun on, or in, the water. Campsites across the United States are commonly located near large bodies of water for just that reason. Some people like to raft, kayak, canoe, or boat. Some waterski, jet ski, or float on air mattresses. Campers who vacation near oceans might even snorkel, paddleboard or surf. And nearly everyone everywhere enjoys the simplest of all water activities: swimming.

Regardless of your chosen activity, there is a good chance your campsite will be located near a body of water.

There might be a lake near your campsite that is perfect for canoeing or kayaking.

OTHER FUN ACTIVITIES

The activities listed above are just a few of the most popular ones campers commonly take part in. The actual number of activities you can do while camping is nearly endless. Other common camping activities include jogging, reading, horseshoes, geocaching, badminton, hide-and-go seek, volleyball, bird-watching, horseback riding, and so much more. They are all so much better than watching television and playing video games.

Anything is better than sitting inside, so why not enjoy geocaching?

ALL GOOD THINGS MUST END

No matter how much fun you are having on your camping adventure, one thing is certain: your trip is going to end. When that time comes, you might be happy to be heading home to your soft bed and more modern surroundings. Or perhaps you would rather camp longer—maybe spend one last day in and out of that favorite swimming hole you found. But the average camping trip lasts just a couple days. Breaking down your campsite so you can head home requires some work, too.

One of the most important unwritten—and sometimes written on big, brown park signs—rules of camping is "leave no trace." This means that your campsite, and every place you visit on your adventure, should be in the same condition it was before you visited.

In their rush to clean up and pack, many campers skip certain important steps. Sure, you may be able to stuff all your belongings into your car in fifteen minutes, but doing so will cost you in the long run. It will make things much more difficult when you arrive home, and also the next time you go camping.

CLEANING UP

The "leave no trace" rule applies to your personal belongings as well. It is important to clean your dishes before you pack them back into your car. Food items should go back into the storage containers you brought them in. Clothes should be zipped up in duffel bags or suitcases. If you used a fire to cook one last meal, it needs to be completely extinguished before you leave.

Next, deflate all sleeping mattresses and roll or fold them up. Roll up your sleeping bag at this time, too. Place both items in the car. If it is raining, most of this packing will be done inside your tent. That is one of the many reasons most campers take down their tent last. Sweep out the inside of the tent first, before taking the tent down in the opposite order in which you installed it. Place all tent materials into the storage bag and place it back into your vehicle. If the tent was damp when you packed it, you will want to take it out when you get home and dry it out. Storing a wet tent will result in mildew forming inside it. It is much easier to dry a tent than it is to remove blackened mildew later.

After the car is packed, take a quick walk across your campsite. The purpose of the walk is to make sure you did not forget anything and also to make sure you picked up every last piece of garbage you may have left. One last rest room break can come in handy, then it is back into the car for the ride home.

DID YOU KNOW?

There are two basic fire types. The first is the teepee which is used to keep a fire in one spot. The second is the crisscross which is used to provide more warmth.

Just as quickly as everything is set up, everything must also be taken down and packed up into the car again.

BACK HOME AGAIN

When your car pulls into your driveway, it may signal the end of your trip but it unfortunately does not mean the chores are all done. You will still need to unload the car, stow your gear, dispose of any garbage you may have brought home, and do the laundry.

This also is the best time to revisit the checklist you put together before you left on your adventure. Were there things you did not use? Cross them off to save time and space next time. Were there supplies that could have made your trip more fun? Add them to the list. Does any of your gear need replaced because it is old or broken? Make note of that, too.

Doing the at-home chores together with family is a great way to reminisce and share memories of the fun times you had together. It is also a good time to plan your next trip. Fortunately, the odds of a next trip happening soon are in your favor. Most campers take several trips a year. There is a reason they do so. The reasons are many, but can be difficult to explain to those who have never camped.

As the father of camping, Thomas Hiram Holding, wrote more than a hundred years ago: "Who can question [campers]? Only those who have never tried it."

FURTHER READING

BOOKS

Brunelle, Lynn. *Camp Out!: The Ultimate Kids' Guide*. New York: Workman Publishing, 2007.

Carlson, Laurie and Judith Dammel. *Kids Camp!: Activities for the Backyard or Wilderness.* Chicago, Illinois: Chicago Review Press, 1995.

Conners, Christine and Tim Conners. *The Scout's Outdoor Cookbook.* Enfield, CT: FalconGuides, 2008.

Drake, Peter G. T*he Complete Practical Guide to Camping, Hiking & Wilderness Skills: Experience The Great Outdoors In Comfort And Safety, From Planning A Trip To Map-Reading And Setting Up Camp.* Leicester, United Kingdom: Southwater, 2014.

Long, Denise. *Survivor Kid: A Practical Guide to Wilderness Survival.* Chicago, Illinois: Chicago Review Press, 2011.

INTERNET ADDRESSES

Campgrounds and Camping Reservations

<www.reserveamerica.com>

Camping, Campsites and Campgrounds

<www.koa.com>

Go Camping America

<www.gocampingamerica.com>

INDEX